Change & Possibility

Change & Possibility
Discovering Hope in Life's Transitions

Text and Photography by
James E. Miller

To Todd and Melanee,
with great respect and even greater love.

ACKNOWLEDGMENTS

I am indebted to William Bridges, whose pioneering work in managing transition has influenced my own thinking. I am grateful to Jacquelyn Holley who unselfishly offered her gathered wisdom, her original thinking, and her editorial assistance in the creation of the audiovisual *Nothing Is Permanent Except Change*, the forerunner to this book. Nancy Frauhiger lent her professional expertise as a psychologist. Clare Barton and Sue Devito provided editorial feedback and proofed the manuscript. My wife Bernie assisted in ever so many ways, as she always does. Katherine Misegades executed the graphic design of this book with her usual flare.

Library of Congress Control Number 2005905662

ISBN 1-885933-38-X

10351 Dawson's Creek Boulevard, Suite B
Fort Wayne, Indiana 46825
260/490-2222
www.willowgreen.com

*Life belongs to the living,
and the one who lives
must be prepared for changes.*

JOHANN WOLFGANG VON GOETHE

Foreword

Let me tell you the story behind this book.

I was in my mid-thirties. I was the minister of a congregation in a medium-size city in the Midwest. Ever since I was a teenager, all I had ever wanted to be was a clergyman. I attended a denominational college and majored in—what else?—religion. I went directly to seminary and earned two advanced degrees. Along the way I got married and had a child. I experienced my share of successes in my work in the parish. I was set.

Then something happened I never planned on. Out of an experience of professional burnout and personal unhappiness, I left the pastoral ministry. In doing so I felt I was leaving behind a large part of myself. In time I also left behind my marriage, much of my security, and many of my dreams.

For a long time I felt quite lost. I didn't know how to handle this terribly difficult time. As I read whatever I could find about going through life changes, I made two discoveries: there wasn't much to read, and most of what I read wasn't all that helpful. I decided that if I made it through my own life change intact, I would one day create something that might help others.

What did I learn? The process took longer than I expected. It hurt as much as I feared. Sometimes the way was as dark as I've ever known. But I also learned this: you can go through a trying time of transition and grow from it. You can be happy again, sometimes happier than you thought possible. You can find meaning in these events and fulfillment in how you respond to these events.

My life is the richer for having made these adjustments through the years, even if I didn't want to make them. My transitions have called from me my better self and have given me blessings I could not have imagined at the time. I still don't look forward to all the changes that come my way and yet I keep learning over and over that change is ultimately my ally.

It is my hope that these pages will help you discover that truth for yourself.

Jim Miller

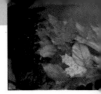

Introduction

You and change are inseparable.

Change alone is eternal, perpetual, immortal.

ARTHUR SCHOPENHAUER

Change is everywhere.

Anything that exists, changes.

Everything that comes into being passes from being.

The universe itself is constantly shifting and moving.

What's true of galaxies is equally true of the earth.

Grasslands turn into deserts,

    and one day are brought back again.

Water overtakes what was once dry land,

    for days at a time, or for eons.

Mountains are born and later they die.

    and as they age, they change shape and even location.

All around us are changes more easily seen,

    more closely experienced:

        winter giving way to spring, summer folding into fall;

           day chasing night, night pursuing day.

All is flux,
nothing is stationary.

HERACLITUS

As the sun's shadow shifts,
so is there no permanence on earth.

AFGHAN PROVERB

We are changing, we have got to change,
and we can no more help it
than leaves can keep from going yellow
and coming loose in autumn.

D. H. LAWRENCE

Change is also within us and others.

Infants turn into toddlers,

   children become adolescents,

      and adults mature in ways no less striking.

New life continually presses to burst forth,

   even as older life presses to burst free.

Yet however much human change is predictable,

   it is equally unpredictable.

Illness strikes, accidents happen, tragedies occur,

   and bodies, minds, and spirits are suddenly changed,

      either for a time or forever.

Relationships come to an end for all sorts of reasons.

Jobs terminate with little or no notice.

People die, expectedly and unexpectedly,

   and life is irreversibly altered for the survivors.

There is no question: in life, change is changeless.

Almost universally, change is uncomfortable.

Even when it is desired, change can be disturbing,

    for it disrupts your normal way of doing things.

It introduces the unknown, the unexperienced.

And when change invades your life

    against your wishes or your will,

        it can jar you even more.

It can leave you feeling disoriented and dispossessed.

It can call into question your abilities and your confidence.

Strong emotions may arise within, ones you'd rather not face,

    ones you may not know *how* to face.

Whatever your changes in life mean to you,

    at one time or another they will create a sense of unease.

They may bring something even more unpleasant—

    pain that refuses to go away.

We change,
whether we like it or not.

RALPH WALDO EMERSON

If we want things to stay as they are,
things will have to change.

GIUSEPPE TOMASI DI LAMPEDUSA

We shrink from change;
yet is there anything
that can come into being
without it?

MARCUS AURELIUS

Contrary to how it may seem,

    you don't have to passively give in to change.

While you cannot always control it,

    you do not have to let change control you.

You have options, always.

Contrary to how you may have visualized it,

    two entirely different processes are at work.

One process is the external change itself,

    usually easily identified.

The other process is the accompanying change

    that happens within you, which we'll call a *transition*.

Every human transition has three distinct phases:

    a beginning, which is also an ending;

        an ending, which is nothing less than a hopeful beginning;

            and in between, a fertile period which may not appear so.

We will begin at the natural starting place—the ending.

I

The beginning of your change
is an ending.

What we call the beginning is often an ending
And to make an end is to make a beginning.
The end is where we start from.

T. S. ELIOT

The beginning of any transition grows out of an ending.

You realize you cannot have what you once had,

   or you can no longer do what you once did.

Something is gone from your life.

Someone you love may have died.

A significant relationship may have come to an end.

You may have lost a part of yourself—

   physical health, emotional well-being, spiritual wholeness.

You may be leaving your job, your home, or your family.

You may be saying farewell to your security or your innocence,

   to well-conceived plans or long-held dreams.

If this change is one you've been looking forward to,

   you may not be expecting any endings at all.

But they're there, just the same,

   whether you see them right away or not.

Every beginning is a consequence.
Every beginning ends something.

PAUL VALERY

The best way out is always through.

ROBERT FROST

Great is the art of beginning,
but greater the art of ending.

HENRY WADSWORTH LONGFELLOW

Whether the change is minor or major,

    whether its effect is fleeting or enduring,

        somewhere at the beginning will be a sense of loss.

And where there is loss, there is grief.

The grief may or may not go deep, but it's grief nonetheless.

While every person grieves differently,

    it's not unusual to experience shock or numbness at first,

        especially if your change is sudden or massive.

Sooner or later you may feel sad or depressed,

    anxious or afraid, slightly irritated or really infuriated.

You may experience fatigue, loneliness, guilt, or shame.

Common also are feelings of relief, gratitude, and joy.

These emotions may come and go quickly, perhaps lightly,

    or they may settle in around you, reluctant to budge.

You may find that you feel few internal responses at all.

Sometimes that happens, too.

Almost universally, the best route is through your feelings,

    not around them.

A wise approach is to honor your feelings,

    not hide them or hide from them.

This approach runs counter to certain popular ideas—

    that a life of happiness can have no room for sadness,

        or that without question gaining is better than losing.

When an ending comes into your life,

    you're given an opportunity to learn otherwise,

        and to show otherwise.

Whatever emotions arise, you can give them their due

    by letting them flow out in ways that are naturally yours.

By speaking your feelings to someone you trust,

    you can gain both perspective and support.

By releasing your emotional energy in healthy ways,

    your life is channeled in healing ways.

Change is not made without inconvenience,
even from worse to better.

RICHARD HOOKER

All changes, even the most longed for,
have their melancholy;
for what we leave behind is a part of ourselves;
we must die to one life before we can enter another.

ANATOLE FRANCE

Wherever we are,
it is but a stage on the way to somewhere else,
and whatever we do, however well we do it,
it is only preparation to do something else
that shall be different.

ROBERT LOUIS STEVENSON

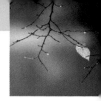

Your future will be influenced by how you undertake change,

so you will do well to maximize your chances for success.

It is important to take care of yourself,

for you need all the strength and stamina you can muster.

So be healthy in your eating and drinking.

Get the exercise you require and the rest you deserve.

Call upon others for help when you need it,

and accept people's offers of assistance when they come.

Put off critical decision-making until it appears the time is right.

In as many ways as you can, trust the process of change.

You may not understand all that's happening or why it's happening,

but you can accept that a valid principle is at work.

Operate under the assumption

that yours is a journey toward growth and healing,

and in time your way will become more clear.

It will.

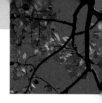

In this time of discontinuity,

    it will help to remember your continuities.

No matter what has changed for you, some things have not changed.

Now is the time to find reassurance in recalling those things.

Whatever inner strength you've already known,

    you can draw on it again.

However resilient you've been, however practical or determined,

    you can be that way once more, for you know how.

You have worked your way through other upheavals in life,

    and you can apply now what you've learned from before.

If someone you love is now gone from your life, others remain,

    and while they cannot replace the one you're missing,

        they can at least be with you as you transition.

And remember, you can turn to that Source of Hope

    who is ready to hold you and lift you even when others do not.

For there is a God who never changes,

    even when everything else appears to.

It is in changing
that things find purpose.

HERACLITUS

Real development is not leaving things behind,
as on a road,
but drawing life from them,
as from a root.

G. K. CHESTERTON

Lord of the world, show me one thing:
Show me what this, which is happening
at this very moment, means to me.

LEVI YITZHAK OF BERDICHEV

Journal.

Buy a notebook. Or use your computer as a journal. Each day write about what's happening—what you're missing, feeling, hoping for. Don't worry about spelling and grammar. Just let what is inside you flow out. Date each entry. Weeks or months later, read back over what you've written. Pick out themes. Highlight turning points. Note your growth. Congratulate yourself on your progress.

Talk with someone.

Talking with another is one of the healthiest things you can do. Find someone with whom you feel comfortable and ask them to listen to what you need to say. People are more inclined to respond positively than you might think, considering it an honor to be asked. Share what you've been going through and how it affects you. You might choose to speak with someone who has been through a similar situation. Is there a support group for you to join? Check with your mental health center, the social work department of your local hospital, or a pastor, priest, or rabbi to learn what the options are. Might an appointment with a professional listener be a good solution? Remember that refusing to talk may slow your progress, and choosing to talk can feel ever so freeing.

Practice relaxation techniques.

Take fifteen or twenty minutes twice a day to relax your whole body. Sit upright in a comfortable straight-backed chair or lie in a quiet place. Uncross your legs and arms. Close your eyes. Breathe slowly and deeply with your diaphragm. Clear your mind little by little each time you exhale. Beginning with your legs, tense the muscles for five seconds and then, while you take ten deep breaths, gradually let the tension out. Do this with your arms, abdomen, chest and shoulders, back, neck and jaw, forehead and scalp.

Repeat this cycle two or three times. Once you feel relaxed, breathe rhythmically for another five minutes before stretching your body and opening your eyes. Another option is to listen to a relaxation audiotape or CD. Certain DVDs may help. Read a book on deep relaxation and experiment until you find what works for you.

Mark your endings.

If you're experiencing the ending of a significant relationship or the loss of something crucial, you may find value in observing this change ritually. Even very short, quiet rituals can be meaningful and healing. Photographs can be mounted and framed. A ring might be ceremonially removed or given away. You might pay a visit to a site that's associated with this ending. You might plant a tree, bush, or flower in remembrance. You might bequeath a possession in gratitude. Ask others to witness any of these rituals if you wish, or do them alone. Either way, your symbolic action can help make real what is ending in your life and be an avenue for your unfolding growth.

Open to the inspirational.

Allow yourself to be lifted by whatever you find inspiring. Many find meaning in reading the Psalms with their enduring themes and honest human expression. Try Psalm 6, 23, 86, 102, and 139. Read the poetic writings of Rumi and Rabindranath Tagore. Dip into some of the classic writers: C.S. Lewis, Thomas Merton, Evelyn Underhill, Thomas Kelly, and Abraham Joshua Heschel, as well as the contemporary ones. Watch an inspiring movie, even if you've seen it several times before. Search out uplifting artwork. Listen to music that feels healing. Let the inspirational guide you, wherever you find it.

II

In between is emptiness—
fertile emptiness.

The night is the mother of the day
The winter of the spring
And even upon old decay
The greenest mosses cling.

JOHN GREENLEAF WHITTIER

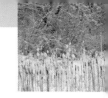

A middle period separates the beginning of a transition

    from its end.

Most likely, you won't know when this period starts.

Phases of change dissolve into one another almost without notice.

They may overlap for awhile.

Yet eventually you'll realize you're in a "between" time.

If the change you're going through is painful and traumatic,

    this period may seem long, arduous, and depressing.

It's like an interminable winter when the cold refuses to leave,

    and the earth is long delayed in its thaw.

The world around you can seem lifeless and dreary,

    and so can your world within.

Even if the change is one you've looked forward to,

    you're likely to experience "in-between" feelings just the same,

        for you must let go of what has been

            before you can fully grasp what will be.

That doesn't happen overnight.

Not until we are lost
do we begin to understand ourselves.

HENRY DAVID THOREAU

One must not always think so much
about what one should do,
but rather what one should be.

MEISTER ECKHART

God, give me grace to accept with serenity
the things that cannot be changed,
the courage to change the things
that should be changed,
and the wisdom to distinguish the one from the other.

REINHOLD NEIBUHR

This middle period will take as long as it takes.

Its duration cannot be foretold,

    no matter what anyone may say.

Two processes are at work here.

One is the external change itself—

    going from being single to being married, for example,

        or from being employed to being unemployed,

            or from being healthy to being ill.

The other process, your internal transition, is altogether different.

Whatever the speed of the changes around you,

    you must go at your own rate through the adjustments within.

Deep within, you are shifting ever so slowly.

Renewal is taking shape ever so gradually.

If you push ahead too quickly,

    you may restrict what's forming inside,

        carefully, fragilely, yet surely.

There is an emptiness to this part of your transition,

a hollowness that contains exactly what you need.

Looking back, you will realize that the key word

for your beginning period was *feeling*.

A main task was to allow yourself to feel whatever welled up.

The key word for this middle time is *being*—just being.

Be in the emptiness, and let it become a temporary home,

as you get used to the reality that the past is past.

Be in the quietness and allow its serenity to soothe you.

Be in the barrenness

and let its austere beauty teach you, comfort you.

Be in the open space that surrounds you,

attending to what is happening within,

to where your desires are leading you.

Be in the moment and savor what it holds.

This may seem less than before,

but it can be enough for now.

Be still, and know that I am God.

PSALM 46:10

Where thou hesitatest between two courses of action,
choose always the one which leaves thee more alone,
more in silence, more in love.

SISTER CONSOLATA

I want to be thoroughly used up when I die,
for the harder I work the more I live.
I rejoice in life for its own sake.
It is a sort of splendid torch
which I have got hold of for the moment,
and I want to make it burn as brightly as possible,
before handing it on to future generations.

GEORGE BERNARD SHAW

You are being given a natural time out.

Poised between the past and the future,

    you're in a position to assess where you've come from

        and to ponder where you're headed.

What has brought you to this place in life?

What do you see now that you didn't see before,

    perhaps *couldn't* see before?

Are you satisfied with the choices you're making?

Do you wish to rethink any of your present decisions?

Now is a fitting time to examine again your priorities.

In light of your recent experiences,

    what is now really important to you?

If you were told your time on earth would soon end,

    what changes would you hurry to make?

What prevents you from turning toward those changes now?

Another opportunity awaits in this "between" time—

to respond soulfully to what is happening around and within.

Since this period shares many characteristics

associated with religious retreats and pilgrimages,

this can be a natural time to go deeper in your spiritual life.

You may experience an aloneness, even if others are around,

for this is *your* transition—no one can go through it for you.

You may find yourself a step removed from everyday routine,

and perhaps far removed, which also makes this time unique.

You may face questions for which you do not yet have answers,

or for which your old answers no longer work.

You may find yourself on a search for something bigger than you.

And in so doing, you may realize this search

is not just for something or someone, but Someone.

With that awareness, your time of change becomes a time

of relating to that which is forever unchanging: the Eternal.

Lord, we know what we are
but not what we shall be.

WILLIAM SHAKESPEARE

So short a time
To teach my life its transpositions to
This difficult and unaccustomed key!

EDNA ST. VINCENT MILLAY

The question is not: why did it happen this way,
or where is it going to lead you,
or what is the price you will have to pay.
It is simply: how are you making use of it?
And about that there is only one who can judge.

DAG HAMMARSKJÖLD

EXPLORATIONS

Visit prior transitions.

Go back over significant changes you've made through the years. List them on paper so you can see them easily. Learn what you can from this list. Have you experienced few or many transitions? How many have been chosen by you and how many dictated for you? How significant have these transitions been? Have any been traumatic? How have you responded in each case? Do you see any pattern in your responses? What helped you through these times? What does all this say about the time you're in now? Gather what you know about yourself as a transitioner.

Take respites.

Even if this is a heavy time for you, you don't have to be weighed down constantly or completely. Give yourself breaks from the pressures and responsibilities. Go to a movie or play, a ball park or a museum. Spend time with people you like. Read something light-hearted. Listen to something entertaining. Watch something amusing. Do something frivolous. When you return from these experiences, you'll not just feel fresher—you'll *be* fresher.

Spend time in nature.

Take long walks outside. Breathe the air slowly. Look around you deliberately. Inspect the trees. Touch the flowers. If you can, lie back to back with the earth and study the clouds. Ponder seeds and sprouts, leaves and limbs, the tiny and the tremendous. Gather lessons as you watch sunrises and sunsets, winter storms and summer rains. You'll find here messages not just about the created world, but about your place in that world. You'll find just as surely a message or two about this transition you're going through.

Inventory your resources.
Be clear about what you have going for you. Get it down in black and white. List the strengths you have that can help you through this time: the skills you've acquired through the years, the traits you've been born with, the advantages you've been given. Name individuals to whom you can turn for specific needs: emotional support, cognitive guidance, tangible assistance, surefire fun. Include your informal networks as well as formal organizations. Keep this list nearby. You can never tell when it will come in handy.

Visualize ideal outcomes.
The only way to get where you want to go is to know where that place is. What do you want your future to look like? In the best of all possible worlds, given what is happening to you, how would you like your days and nights to be spent? Where would you live? How would you work? Who would be included in your life? What would add meaning to your days? Start visualizing your ideal as a guide for when it's time to make your way to the real.

Make a retreat.
Get away somewhere and make room for your soul to listen and speak. Spend a few days at a monastery in quietness. Attend a weekend event at a retreat center. If you're hesitant to go by yourself, ask a friend to go with you. Locate a spiritual director in your area and spend time with that person on a regular basis.

III

At the end of your transition
is a new beginning.

And yes I said yes I will Yes!

JAMES JOYCE

Internal beginnings have a way of creeping up on you.

One moment they're not there, the next they are.

They may come with a quiet rustle or a whisper,

> or they may announce themselves with fanfare.

However they make themselves known, beginnings carry with them

> an energy that is unmistakable and a promise that is undeniable.

For, as much as anything, beginnings are life's way of saying "Yes!"

Yes, whatever has happened, something new can occur.

Yes, whatever is gone, something original can appear,

> or something significant can reappear.

And, yes, this occurs not just around you, but within you.

Your beginnings are no more important than your endings,

> no more worthwhile than your interim time.

They're simply the next step in your growth,

> another chance to become more completely

>> who you're meant to be.

*We must always change, renew, rejuvenate ourselves;
otherwise we harden.*

JOHANN WOLFGANG VON GOETHE

*The real voyage of discovery consists
not in seeking new landscapes
but in having new eyes.*

MARCEL PROUST

*There is nothing more difficult to take in hand,
more perilous to conduct,
or more uncertain in success,
than to take the lead in the introduction
of a new order of things.*

INSCRIPTION ON MACHIAVELLI'S TOMB

You'll note a shift in this last period of your transition.

While the first phase emphasized *feeling*,

and the second, *being*,

the emphasis now is upon *doing*.

You'll recognize this time when it appears:

you'll feel drawn to doing what comes next,

what comes naturally.

The clearing away will have gone on long enough.

Now comes the time to add, to build, to move ahead.

Now comes the energy to repair, to create, to launch out.

These new beginnings are enticing.

They beckon you to follow your longings.

And these are not your old longings,

for those will have changed as a result of all you've been through.

Beginnings invite you to give substance to heartfelt dreams,

which can wait no longer to become reality.

Beginnings tend to capture your imagination—they're fun.

They evoke the child in you, whatever your age.

They bring out the creative part of you—

    the artist or the poet,

        the minstrel or the clown.

Joy will reawaken in you, deepened by your experience.

Hope will blossom anew, strengthened by this journey.

Your sense of wonder will reappear, unveiling the world.

But there's more to your beginnings than enjoyment—

    often they take work.

You may have to immerse yourself in details

    and follow step-by-step through procedures.

You may have to do what you don't want to do,

    or don't know how to do, or fear to do.

Yet deep in your heart you know it's right to move ahead.

The time has come.

Patient endurance
Attains all things.

TERESA OF AVILA

Weeping may linger for the night,
but joy comes with the morning.

PSALM 30:5

When old words die out on the tongue,
new melodies break forth from the heart;
and where the old tracks are lost,
new country is revealed with its wonders.

RABINDRANATH TAGORE

As your vitality resurfaces,

   you may be inclined to rush ahead.

Wisdom offers this counsel: not too fast.

This is a time to pace yourself,

   learning what there is to learn as you go,

      savoring what there is to savor along the way.

It's a time to proceed gently, leniently, graciously.

Remember: beginnings do not always go easily.

Trials may lead to errors—that's to be expected.

Exertion may cause fatigue—that's only natural.

Also, this is a time to be sensitive to others,

   those undergoing their own changes,

      and those adjusting to yours.

Ultimately, it is a time to accept responsibility for yourself:

   for the part you've played in making you who you are,

      and for the part you're playing in who you're becoming.

It's difficult to make sense of all that is happening,

    right as it happens.

This final phase will give you a viewpoint that can help you.

Over the course of time, and through the eyes of experience,

    you'll be able to see patterns in your responses.

You'll be able to identify problems that were solved,

    answers that were found,

        and solutions you can hold onto until another time.

You can start to understand how *this* happened and not *that*,

    and even if you cannot fully comprehend it,

        at least you can move toward accepting it.

You can make your own way down that path toward meaning.

As you do so, you can honor the mystery that life so often holds,

    making a place for that mystery in your own life.

You can abide with the unknown,

    confident that the Unknowable already abides with you,

        and always will.

Weep not that the world changes—did it keep
A stable, changeless state, it were cause indeed to weep.

WILLIAM CULLEN BRYANT

A Death blow is a Life blow to Some
Who till they died did not alive become—
Who had they lived, had died but when
They died, Vitality begun.

EMILY DICKINSON

As the hand is made for holding
and the eye for seeing,
Thou hast fashioned me for joy.
Share with me the vision
that shall find it everywhere.

GAELIC PRAYER

Explorations

Encourage creativity.
The last phase of your transition is easily the most creative. Brainstorm all the options you can think of, even the dumb ones. Ask the most imaginative people you know to feed you ideas. Do your dreaming in a place new to you, a place you enjoy. Make simple changes in how you do things. For example, use your opposite hand. Draw with those great big crayons. Paint with a small friend's watercolors. Expect something new to come to you and it will.

Ask for feedback.
If your transition has been long in unfolding, you'll find it helpful to get another perspective. Ask someone who knows you well to describe how they see you now, compared to the way you used to be. Which changes are most obvious? What has impressed them about how you've handled this time? What input do they have about this new path of yours? Remember: not everyone will understand your changes. And don't forget this rule from the medical world: it's okay to get second and third opinions.

Write a dialogue.
Once you're well into your new beginning, compose a conversation between "Old Me" and "New Me." Have them talk to each other about what has happened. What does each want the other to know? Just scribble the first things that come to mind. Write until the dialogue has ended. Then read aloud what the two have said. What is there to affirm about Old Me? About New Me? Save what you've written and read it again in six months.

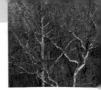

Tell your story.
Stories are powerful. They're also popular—everyone likes a good yarn. So go ahead: tell yours. Weave the entire tale of this transition of yours as only you can weave it. Tell it in words or tunes, with paint or film, with whatever best suits you and your theme. Compile a scrapbook. Edit a video. Do this for yourself if for no one else. You may be surprised how many people will find meaning in learning your story.

Share yourself.
You're in a unique position to help others who are in the midst of change. Because you've survived and grown through your experience, you can do more than just help—you can be an inspiration. Offer what your experience tells you they might need. Perhaps you have practical information that will assist. Perhaps you can give them your listening ear, your knowing assurance. Share the most valuable resource you have: yourself.

Take something with you.
As you move on to other parts of your life, take this experience with you. Find or create a symbol that reminds you of what has happened and what you do not want to forget. Place your symbol on a mantel or table or dashboard, or carry it on a necklace or key chain, or in your pocket or purse. Experiences of transition are too important to be left behind. Take yours with you into your future.

Conclusion

Change will not change,
but you can.

There is nothing in this world constant,
but inconstancy.

JONATHAN SWIFT

Change is here to stay.

It will always accompany you,

 because you are the way you are,

  because life is the way life is.

There will continually be losses for you to accommodate,

 and endings for you to negotiate.

The unexpected will find you wherever you are,

 as will the unplanned and the unwanted.

New beginnings will come your way,

 whether they're given *to* you or fashioned *by* you.

Whatever the reasons for all these shifts in your life,

 you will not be able to avoid them.

You cannot stop change.

But that does not mean you're helpless in the face of change,

 or that you have no choices in the matter.

For you have one freedom that can never be taken from you.

The choice is always ours.

ALDOUS HUXLEY

If fate throws a knife at you,
there are two ways of catching it—
by the blade and by the handle.

ORIENTAL PROVERB

Everything can be taken away from a person
but one thing: the last of human freedoms—
to choose one's attitude
in any given set of circumstances,
to choose one's own way.

VICTOR FRANKL

You are free to choose how you'll respond to change in your life.

You may elect to see it always and only as a threat.

Or you may decide to explore whatever possibilities come with it,

    as small or uncertain as they may seem at the time.

You may choose to read each change as a sign of danger.

Or you may look to see if a note of invitation is hidden within.

You may treat your transitions as problems that must be borne.

Or you may regard them as challenges that can be enriching.

The way you choose to see the changes around you

    will help determine the impact they leave upon you.

And the way you approach the necessary transitions within you

    will help determine how your life unfolds from those points,

        and whether those times become times of growth.

These are decisions only you can make.

Clearly, such decisions are not without risks.

Fortunately, the risks are worth it.

Whether change chooses you or you choose change,

    it can bring you fresh perspective and new options.

You can learn to be more flexible and resilient

    while you become more capable and versatile.

You can become more self-aware and self-assured.

You can increase your knowledge about others,

    while you also increase your concern, your compassion,

        and ultimately your love.

You can treat your times of change as wake-up calls,

    inviting you to look again at your values and priorities,

        to become clearer about what's truly important

            for the living of the days you're given on earth.

You can uncover significant life lessons you'll always remember.

In other words, you can set the stage

    to do what a time of change so naturally encourages:

        make a fresh beginning.

Change is the nursery
Of music, joy, life, and eternity.

JOHN DONNE

I find the great thing in this world
is not so much where we stand,
as in what direction we are moving.

OLIVER WENDELL HOLMES

If I take the wings of the morning
and settle at the farthest limits of the seas,
even there your hand shall lead me,
and your right hand shall hold me fast.

PSALM 139:9-10

By now it's clear: yours is not just a time of transition—

yours is a life of transitions.

One change will follow another as long as you live,

and some will not wait to follow—

they will perch one right on top of another.

You will learn as you go,

doing your own changing on the spot.

You will find companionship along the way

because, unique as your changes may be,

change is not unique to you—

you are in good company.

And you will experience first-hand this truth:

in all the changes of your life, there is something unchangeable.

Whatever comes, Someone never leaves you.

And whatever leaves you, Someone always remains.

Always.

I do dimly perceive
that whilst everything around me
is ever changing, ever dying,
there is underlying all that change
a living power that is changeless,
that holds all together,
that creates, dissolves, and recreates.
That informing power of spirit is God.
And since nothing else that I see
merely through the senses can or will persist,
God alone is.

MAHATMA GANDHI

BOOKS BY JAMES E. MILLER

Autumn Wisdom

When Mourning Dawns

A Pilgrimage Through Grief

How Will I Get Through the Holidays?

What Will Help Me?/How Can I Help?

Winter Grief, Summer Grace

One You Love Has Died

When You're Ill or Incapacitated/When You're the Caregiver

The Caregiver's Book: Caring for Another, Caring for Yourself

When You Know You're Dying

One You Love Is Dying

When A Man Faces Grief/A Man You Know Is Grieving

Finding Hope: Ways to See Life in a Brighter Light

The Art of Being a Healing Presence

The Art of Listening in a Healing Way

My Shepherd Is the Lord

Effective Support Groups

The Rewarding Practice of Journal Writing

And others.

VIDEO PROGRAMS BY JAMES E. MILLER

Invincible Summer

Listen to Your Sadness

How Do I Go On?

Common Bushes Afire

By the Waters of Babylon

Why Yellow?

Nothing Is Permanent Except Change

We Will Remember

Gaining A Heart of Wisdom

The Grit and Grace of Being a Caregiver

Awaken to Hope

Be at Peace

The Natural Way of Prayer

You Shall Not Be Overcome

When Mourning Dawns

All Seasons Shall Be Sweet

My Shepherd Is The Lord

Still Waters

The Art of Listening in a Healing Way

And others.

James E. Miller is a writer, photographer, spiritual director, workshop leader, and speaker who creates resources and gives presentations in the areas of loss, transition, caregiving, healing presence, spirituality, and older age. He is a frequent speaker before many professional groups and at various institutions, often incorporating his own award-winning photography. He leads workshops and conducts retreats throughout North America.

To discuss bringing him to your area, call 260/490-2222 or email *jmiller@willowgreen.com*.